JOURNAL TO THE SOUL FOR TEENAGERS

ROSE OFFNER

This book belongs to

AMANDA CABRAL

It is my private journal.
Thank you for honoring my request.
Please do not read it without my permission.

CELESTIAL
Berkeley, California

CELESTIALARTS

P.O. Box 7123
Berkeley, California 94707
e–mail: order@tenspeed.com
website: www.tenspeed.com

Celestial Arts books are distributed in Canada by Ten Speed Canada,
in the United Kingdom and Europe by Airlift Books, in New Zealand
by Southern Publishers Group, in Australia by Simon & Schuster Australia,
in South Africa by Real Books, and in Singapore, Malaysia, Hong Kong,
and Thailand by Berkeley Books.

A Heart & Star Book
ISBN 0–89087–899–4

First printing, 1999
Printed in Hong Kong

05 04 03 02 01 00 99 / 1 2 3 4 5 6

Acknowledgments

This book was inspired by my daughter, Danielle Offner-DeGroot, whose challenges in finding and being true to herself have led us both on a journey to our souls, expressing our anger, hurt, pain, and disappointments and then reconciling and coming to a place of love again.

Rick Bowman, my best friend and husband, gives me strength and inspiration and supports my creative endeavors. I love you.

And to my mother, Casia Ruiz, I can't tell you how sorry I am for all the grief I caused you when I was a teenager. Now I understand. I love you, Mom.

This is also for my nieces and nephews who are also teenagers, I love you all and am so proud of you. Samantha Smith, Eric Smith, Craig Gilmore, Ryan Gilmore, Andrew Ruiz, Cara Bowman, Chelsea Bowman, Chad Bowman, Ashley Caldwell, and Blake Caldwell. This is also for my sweet niece Chelsea Ruiz, who isn't a teenager yet, but who is my little sweetheart.

Thanks to Redwood Alternative School in Castro Valley, California, for allowing me to test the exercises and get their students' valuable feedback. Thanks to principal Diana Levy, Catherine Rothrock, and all the English students in attendance.

To the great teachers from Proviso West High School in Hillside, Illinois, who shared themselves and their insights with me: James Brakie, Mara Goodman, Tara Leonard, Hal Tarr, and Angela Strater. And to my friend Debra Rose for always taking care of me while I'm in Chicago. Your hospitality and creative input are so appreciated.

And to Gloria Carson, teacher at Modesto High School and Fred C. Byer High School in Modesto, California, who encouraged my work with teenagers and invited me to speak at Byer High.

A special thanks to Jennifer Bowman and Erin McCole for their wonderful insights. Congratulations and best wishes as you enter into your adult life.

Thanks to all of the teenagers who so willingly allowed me to interview them at Jamie Taddei's graduation party; Jamie, I love you, and I am so proud of you. Thank you, Corinne Zuleger, Alisha Bolar, Nicole Sanderson, Kristen Nolan, and Megan O'Toole.

A big thanks to Dan, Crystal Stultz, Jayonna, Tiffany, and to those of you whom I may have left out but gave me your help.

A big thanks to Matthew Taylor and to all the teenagers who reviewed the manuscript and gave me their insightful comments.

A special thanks to Elizabeth Barker of Temporarily Yours, for your organizational assistance. It was much needed and appreciated.

Thanks to JoAnn Deck, editor at Celestial Arts, for believing in, supporting, and holding the vision of creating positive change. Your hard work, patience, and dedication are invaluable. And Kathryn Ettinger, thank you and congratulations on your heartfelt edits.

Veronica Randall, art director and creative soul, thanks for your wonderful brainstorms and artistic vision. And to my publisher, Phil Wood, a heartfelt thanks. And an emotional thanks to David Hinds, who is sorely missed; you have touched my life. All of us at Ten Speed miss you.

I thank God for giving me the inspiration and the fortitude to keep going and to work from my heart.

Contents

I yearn to hear and to live in accordance with the Voice that speaks from my heart and whispers in the trees.

I yearn to feel my feelings, to accept my beauty, and to love myself for the magnificent being that I truly am.

I yearn for the compassion to forgive myself, and for the compassion and understanding to forgive those who I believed have harmed me.

I yearn to wake each morning and be thankful for the gift of life, to view others in my life with gratitude for the gifts they bring to me that I might learn and grow and remember.

I yearn to cry and to cry and to cry that I may wash away the pain and bitter sorrow that feasts on my soul, and to cry again, to cleanse the wounds of the lost child within me.

I yearn to know and believe that I am as deserving as any child of God of the richness and abundance provided by the Divine, and for the willingness and courage to accept and experience that richness and abundance.

I yearn for joy and happiness and the wisdom of all the dead poets.

I yearn to be sensitive to the needs of others, to hear their cries, to recognize and acknowledge the gifts that I bring to this life, and to selflessly give of myself in the service of humanity.

I yearn to be humble and to accept responsibility for the conditions of my life.

I yearn to be more sensitive to the needs of my own soul, to honor those needs, and to be less vulnerable to the petty demands of my ego.

I yearn for the freedom and spontaneity to dream and imagine, to expand my vision of life.

I yearn to release my perception of the haunting memories of the past, and I pray for the courage to surrender to the love that is within.

I yearn to travel, to explore distant lands, to meet the wonderful peoples of the world.

I yearn to share in their celebrations, to eat their foods, to sing their songs and to dance their dance.

— Jack Newton

Introduction

The Heart of the Matter

Growing up isn't easy. Being a teenager is one of the most difficult passages of life, often filled with uncertainty, pain, and a deep need for love and acceptance. Our family history influences our life. This journal was inspired by my own teenage daughter and her challenges, the memory of my own struggles, and the story of my mother's life.

I was born to a young girl of sixteen and by the time she was nineteen, there were three of us. She divorced my father when I was a baby and married my stepfather, who raised me. I never felt truly loved or accepted by my stepfather. The truth is we didn't much like each other, especially when I was a teenager. He always said no to everything. We fought constantly and the tension between us affected my growth as well as my relationship with myself and others. Finally I chose to forgive him and my life has been much better since.

Sometimes it feels like there is no one who understands you and you cannot even understand yourself. Your journal is the place to express your fears, challenges, love,

sadness, and joy. It is the place to write about yourself, your family, your friends, your hopes, and your dreams.

The gold border on the cover of this book is embedded with jewels to remind us of our own precious nature. The clouds represent the hopes and dreams we strive for. The castle symbolizes the fulfillment of the journey we take to attain our goals and dreams. This book acts as a map for finding, fulfilling, and honoring your true spirit.

SELF-INQUIRY is the practice of honest examination, in which we learn to ask ourselves some of life's hardest questions. We all desire love and acceptance, but until we have made peace with ourselves, it is difficult to have loving relationships with our family and friends. Knowing and being true to ourselves is one of the greatest gifts we can give ourselves and others. Keeping a journal is a valuable tool for self–discovery.

Relationships with FAMILY AND FRIENDS present some of life's great challenges. Belonging to a group and trying to fit in and still find a way to be true to yourself can be very difficult. You can feel alone, even in your own family. Perfect families exist only in our imaginations. Parents sometimes make mistakes, mistakes that can take time to heal. Some teenagers practically have to raise themselves with little or no help from anyone. Challenges like this can affect self–esteem, our ability to love, and sometimes even the ability to discern right from wrong. Writing about the family challenges we face and giving thanks for the good things we have can help us to find our way in life.

Sometimes our friends can understand us when our families can't and they can give us a sense of belonging. But most of us have also experienced betrayal by someone we thought was a friend. In time we come to find and know who our true friends are. Real friends do not bring us down, but encourage us to be better than we are. To be called a friend is one of the greatest compliments you can receive. Friendship creates a circle of love and support that can endure the test of time. Some people are fortunate enough to have friendships within their own family; for others, their friends have nurtured them and become like family to them.

As we move FROM ANGER AND HURT TO FORGIVENESS, we come to recognize that unexpressed emotions can turn into rage. Alcohol, drug abuse and destructive behaviors are often acts of anger and pain which have been turned inward against ourselves. We all have parts of ourselves that we may not like and desire to change.

Having a safe place to express ourselves begins the journey to healing our deepest sorrows. Writing can make us feel very vulnerable, so you might find yourself crying as you begin to express yourself. When this happens, stay with your feelings without repressing them. When we cry we are admitting the pain. As we express ourselves our true feelings come out, and we begin to heal our past.

Writing about our anger and pain helps us to let go of our hurt, and we can begin to forgive. Forgiveness creates a release of negative energy. As we forgive, our hearts open and our capacity to love increases.

FINDING YOUR VOICE leads us on the path to being true to ourselves. Sharing ourselves with those we love helps them to know us. Often when we share our stories and our fears what we really want is to be heard. Choosing the right time to share our thoughts and feelings is critical. Talking, listening, acknowledging, and being fully present are the tools for finding and sharing our voice. Expressing ourselves out loud can lead us to our passion, what we truly believe in, and our unique and special gifts.

In THE ART OF LOVE, you will find a place to explore your feelings about what it means to be loved. We all want to be loved and accepted. Yet in order to be loved, we must first love ourselves. Good self-esteem is created by honoring and respecting ourselves and taking care of our responsibilities.

If we grew up without positive role models, we may not have learned how to love ourselves and others. Respect for ourselves and for others can be easily lost. Yet as we come to respect ourselves, others will also respect us.

Our hearts have their own intelligence. All we have to do is listen. When we are confronted with something that violates our values, we feel it deep inside. Many teenagers experience pressures that contradict the voice in their heart. The more we listen to ourselves and love ourselves, the more we are able to give and receive love.

CHALLENGES, CHANGE, AND GROWTH are a natural part of growing up. Each and every experience we have changes us. Being true to ourselves and overcoming the pressures we face in our lives can be confusing. Yet if we ask with an open heart and listen carefully, the answers are always there. Keeping a journal as a chronicle of your life can prevent you from making the same mistakes over and over again. Often by the time you finish writing about a problem or question you have, the answer has made itself known to you.

On the JOURNEY TO YOUR HEART'S DESIRES, imagination and passion are vital ingredients for turning dreams into reality. We all have dreams and we all deserve the opportunity to make our dreams come true. Taking action releases us from our fears and resistance and moves us in the direction of our heart's desires. Doing what we are passionate about gives us a sense of fulfillment. As we keep our agreements with ourselves and others, our dreams begin to come true. This journal becomes your blueprint for designing your life.

How to Begin

Journal to the Soul for Teenagers will inspire curiosity, so find a safe place to keep it. Be sure not to leave your journal lying around where someone might be tempted to read it. If your privacy is ever violated, don't stop writing. You can put anything you don't want anyone to read in a sealed envelope and then in a special pocket that you can create and glue into your journal. It is a way of ensuring your privacy.

Write directly over the art. Your written word enhances the images and makes the pages look even more beautiful. Be sure to make a mistake as fast as you can and just get it over with. Some of my favorite pieces of art came out of what seemed like mistakes, just as some of my greatest life lessons have also come from mistakes.

If you are uncertain about your writing style and worried that you tend to ramble when you write, simply ask yourself what you are really trying to say, and then say it. Try to get to the point of the issue at hand.

Decorating Your Journal

You can embellish your journal with stickers, collage, artist-quality construction paper (for pockets), gold pens (they sometimes leak, so be careful), colored pens and pencils, glitter glue, Crayola Overwriters™, and Crayola Changeables™.

If there isn't enough writing space in an exercise, simply continue on with another sheet of paper, title it, and put it into a pocket that you can create and place anywhere in the book. Gluing pockets and envelopes into your journal is one way to begin claiming it and making it your own.

To make a pocket, simply cut a piece of paper in half, preferably a piece of construction paper or heavier-weight paper and glue the bottom and sides only. You now have a special place to put your private feelings or your treasured keepsakes. You can design and use lots of different pockets and envelopes in this journal:

AN ANGER POCKET–a place to write about your anger and frustration. Writing on separate pieces of paper and putting them in the anger pocket allows you to write with emotional abandon about the things you wouldn't want to permanently put in the pages of your journal. You can later throw these pieces of paper away or keep them until you have resolved the issue within yourself.

A GARBAGE BAG—a pocket to express and then throw away your negative thoughts, doubts, fears, or anything that someone has said or done that hurt you. This can help you let go of the past, along with your anger.

AN IMAGE POCKET—a holder for you to save favorite images from magazines or cards. Write about these images and explain why you are attracted to them, or create designs or make collages with them.

A LOVE POCKET—a place to keep your favorite letters, cards, ticket stubs, or anything you cherish. As you grow and change this pocket will always hold a special place in your heart.

A GOOD FORTUNES POCKET—a place for saving favorite fortunes from fortune cookies or for writing your own, as you begin to affirm your good fortune in life.

For Your Continued Journey

A GIFT OF MORE EXERCISES appears at the back of the book to encourage you to create your own journal once you have completed this book. If there is an exercise you can't relate to or don't like, or if you

have blank pages because you needed less writing space for an exercise, you can choose one of these extra exercises, or you can make up your own questions for yourself. Keep in mind that whatever exercise you don't want to do is often the exercise you would benefit from doing most. I send you strength and the courage to be true to yourself and follow your dreams.

As a teenager I struggled with my parents. Now I am a parent, and my daughter struggles with me as well as herself. I wrote this for her and for you, that you might find your own way, with your own words.

Rose Offner

11

My True Self

Write about your true self. Describe how you see yourself and how others see you. Who can you be your true self with?

Metamorphosis

Describe the changes you are going through. How are you different than you were a year ago? Two years ago? Who are you becoming?

Great Expectations

Write about your talents, skills, and strengths. What do you do well and how might this become part of your future? Write about why you are so great and what makes you special.

The Steps

Name your top three goals. Think realistically, and list the actions you would need to take in order to achieve your dreams and desires.

In Style

Describe the way you dress and your personal style.
How does your style affect your attitude?
Does the way you dress affect how people see you or
how you see others?

Looking Inside

When you look at yourself, what do you see?
What are the things you like or dislike about
yourself? How can you feel more confident or accepting
of yourself? Describe your best features or attributes.

Totally Private

Sometimes we have secrets and we are afraid to tell anyone. Write about your private thoughts. Include something that is bothering you and you need to express. For privacy, you can write these thoughts on a separate piece of paper, which you can throw away or tuck in an envelope that you glue here.

Random
Acts
of Courage

Our fears keep us stuck. Name your fears. What actions could you take to face your fears and build a courageous heart?

Learning About Love

Express what you have learned about relationships from your parents, grandparents, caregivers, or other family members. Describe what you have learned about love.

Family Matters

Families are people who love you. You might live with both parents, a single parent, stepparents, grandparents, or adoptive parents, or you might live in a unique family situation. Describe your family. Are you close? Do you get along? What challenges do you face?

Life at Home

Describe your home life in detail. Who do you live with? What is your room like? Write about your ideal home life. What are you thankful for? What would you change if you could?

Knowing You

Write about whether your family really knows you. What prevents them from knowing you better?

Yes and No

What do your parents say yes to and no to and what are their reasons? What happens when they say no? How do you negotiate?

Circle of Friends

Real friends support you, accept you, and appreciate who you are. List the qualities of a true friend. Write about your closest friends and describe how they bring out the best or the worst in you. Describe what makes you a good friend.

44

Betrayal

Have you ever been betrayed by someone you thought was a friend? Express the way or ways you have been betrayed and how this has affected you, your ability to trust, and your current relationships with others, or write about a time you betrayed someone.

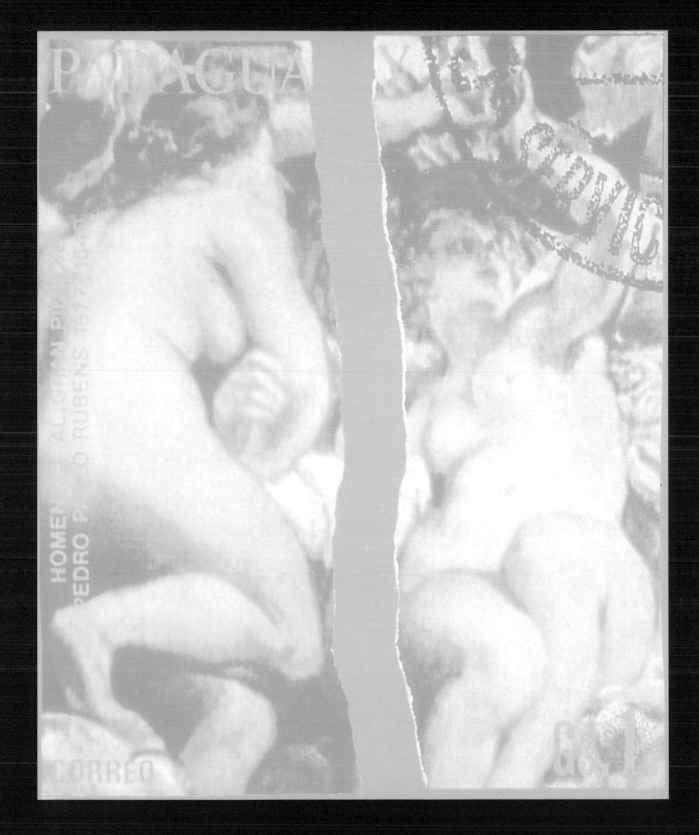

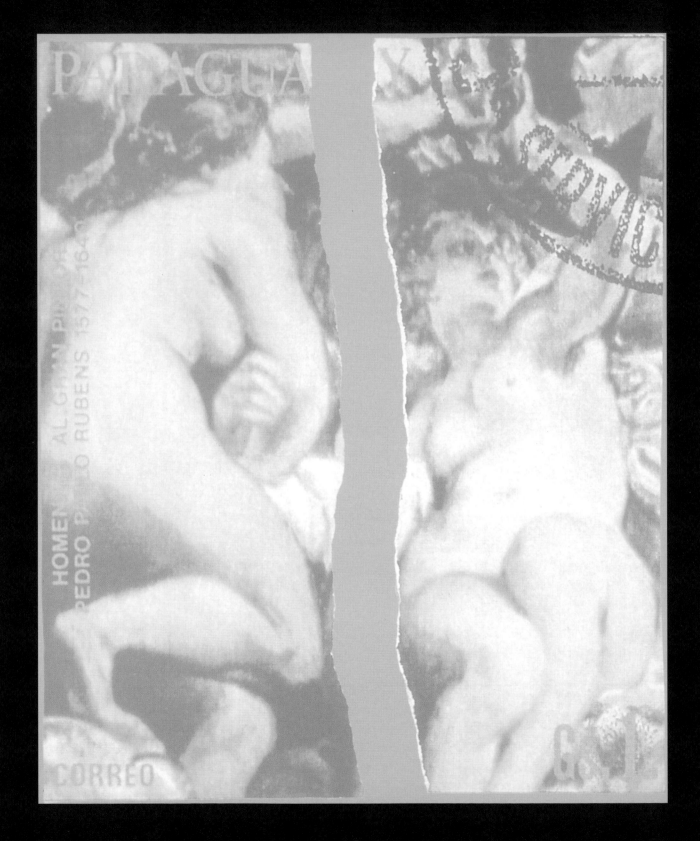

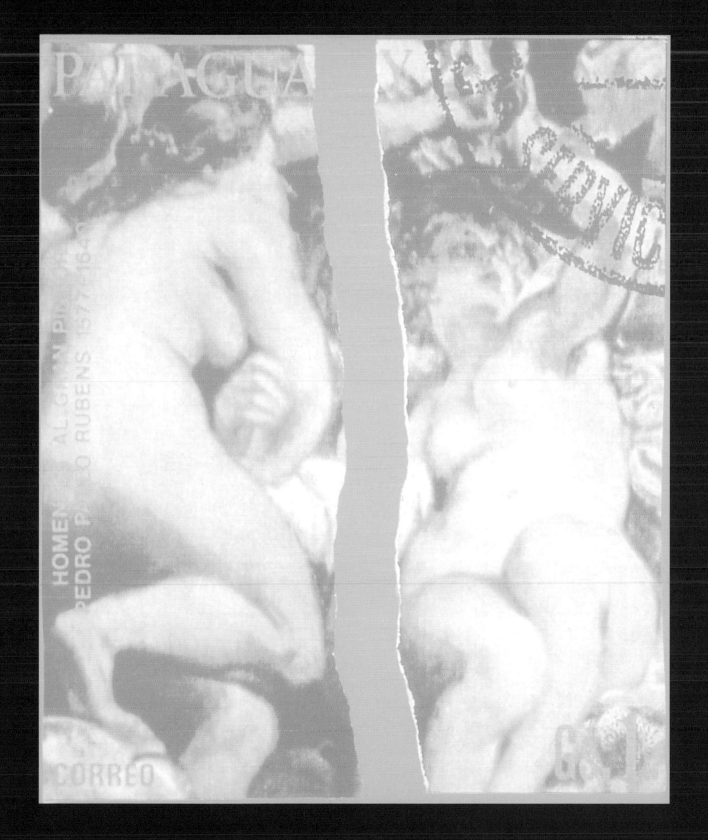

Curiosity and Pressure

How does pressure affect the everyday choices you make? Have you ever been in a situation that is uncomfortable, that left you feeling pressured to do something you didn't want to do? How did you react? How did it make you feel? Would you do it differently if you were in the same situation again? Think about how you can deal with your own curiosity and the pressure and influence of others.

Parties

Describe your experiences at parties. Have you been around drugs, drinking, and smoking? How do you handle yourself in these situations? Have you felt pressured to do something you're not comfortable with in order to be accepted? What can you do in that kind of situation?

Endings

Write about a friendship or a relationship that ended. Describe what happened and how it has affected you.

It Hurts

Write about the times in your life when you have been hurt. Who hurt you? Describe how these experiences have affected you.

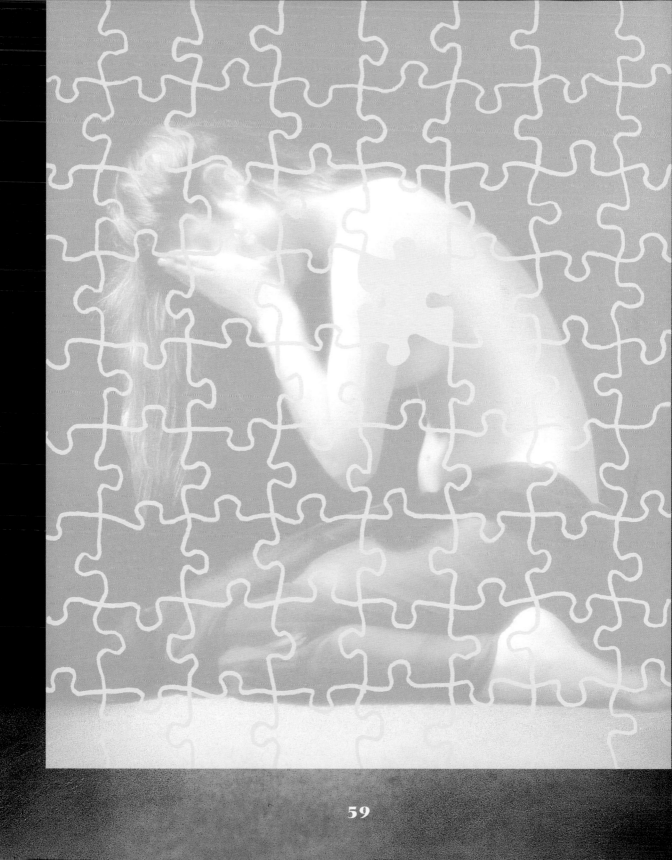

Hurting Others

Write about the people you have hurt and what you did to hurt them. Why did you do it? How did it make you feel? This is a good beginning for making amends to others.

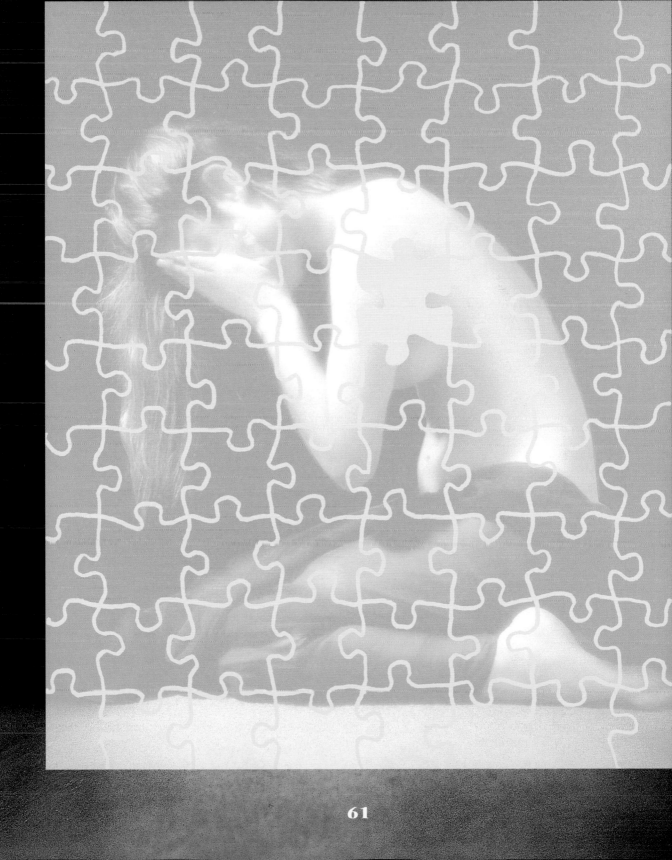

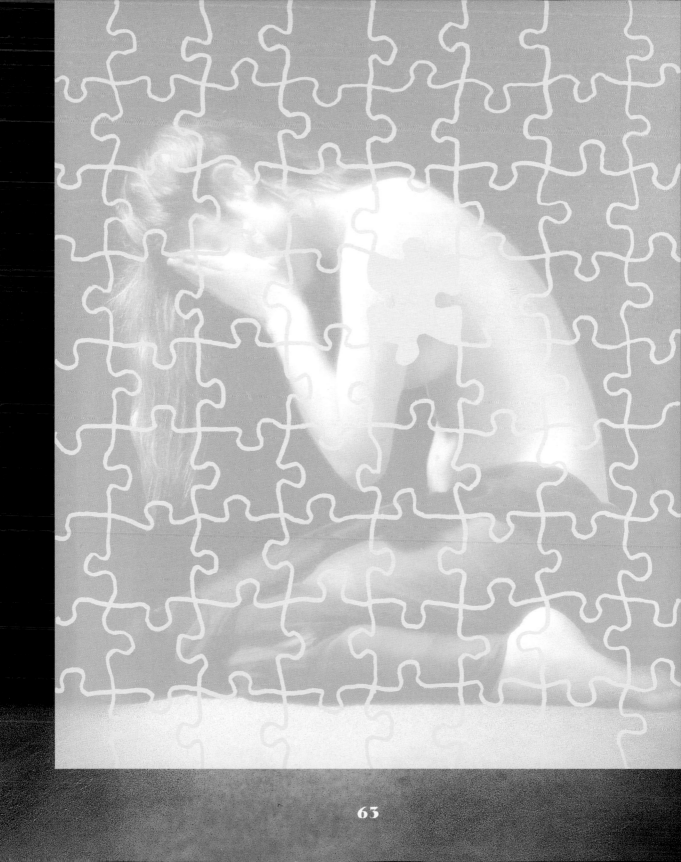

Anger and Rage

Our anger often has a history. Unexpressed anger can turn into rage and dangerous behavior that can hurt us and those around us. Expressing our feelings clears the air.

Think of a situation or person that has made you angry. Recall the situation or person clearly. Identify what the other person said or did and list the feelings this memory evokes. Were you hurt, scared, or frustrated?

What do you need to do in order to take care of yourself?

Go back to your first memory of what happened and how it made you feel. Go back as far as you can, recalling if you had any childhood memories of these or similar feelings. Imagine yourself doing whatever you needed to do in order to take care of yourself. Any time you feel anger, remember to ask yourself, "How am I not taking care of myself right now?" and do whatever you need to do to take care of yourself, stand up for yourself, or express yourself.

Garbage

Make a garbage bag pocket from a brown paper bag and glue it here. On a separate piece of paper, write about the garbage you carry around with you: your negative thoughts, doubts, fears, anything that is holding you back from happiness. Now throw them away here.

Grace and Forgiveness

Write an unsent letter to someone who has angered you or hurt you, someone you perhaps would like to forgive but don't know how. Write the letter in your journal and don't send it, or write it on another piece of paper and make an unsent letter pocket. Often after we write an unsent letter we experience a release or a feeling of peace or resolution.

Answers from Above

Imagine that your Guardian Angel, God, or your Higher Power is writing you a letter about your current challenge. Close your eyes, take a deep breath, open your eyes, and begin writing. Receive your answers from the heart.

Stamp

Gratitude

It is said that whatever we are thankful for will increase in our lives. Keep an ongoing list of everything you are grateful for in your life.

Talking, Listening, and Hearing

Who can you talk to? Who really listens to you and hears you? Who doesn't hear or listen to you? How does this affect you? Make a list of what you would like to tell those who are not listening so that they might understand what you're feeling and who you are.

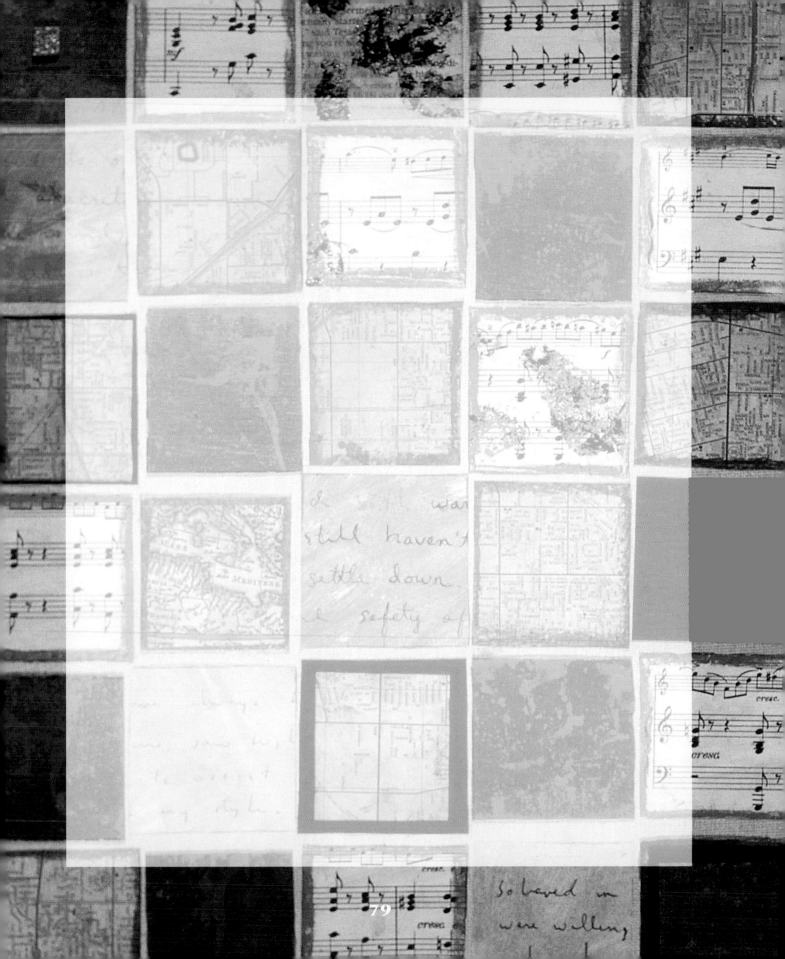

Life's Teachers

Describe someone who has affected your life in a positive way, a teacher, a role model, a friend. Write about how they believed in you, inspired you, or saw the best in you.

Truth and Lies

The truth is liberating—it frees our minds, hearts, and souls.
Yet sometimes we are not honest even with ourselves.
Who do you lie to and why? Who do you tell the truth to?
What lies do you tell your parents, your friends, yourself?
Why aren't you telling the truth, and what would happen if you did?

82

Rebellion

Describe the ways you rebel. What are you rebelling against and why? How is this affecting your friendships, family life, and they way you view yourself?

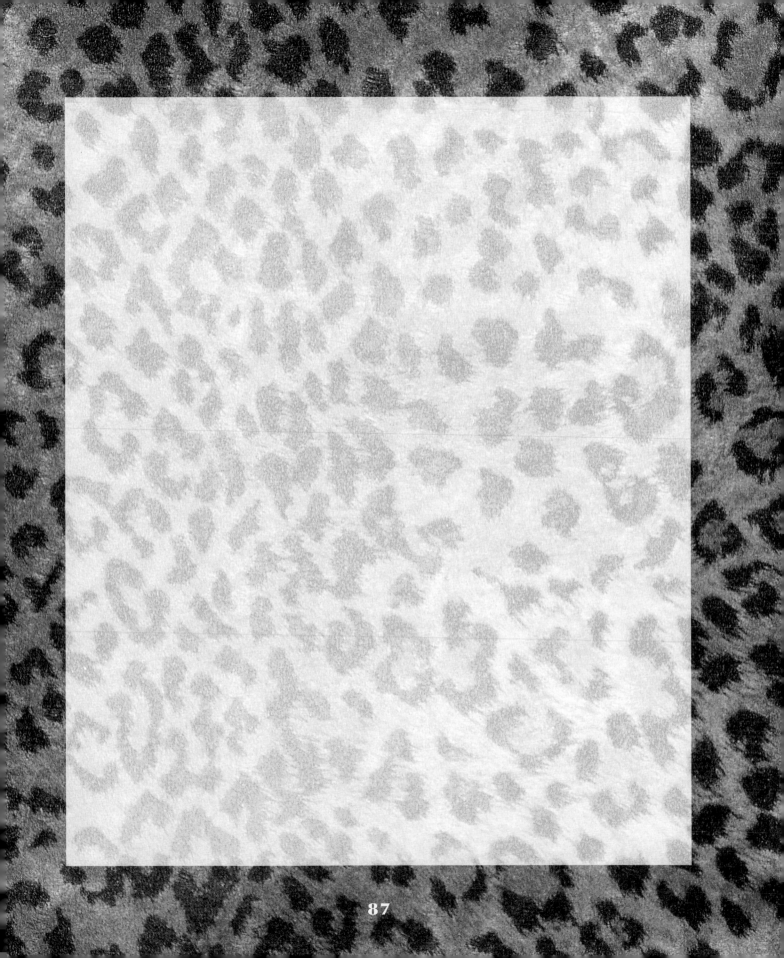

Flying Words

Often when you are fighting with those you love, you are really angry at yourself. Underneath our anger is often disappointment. Who are you fighting with? What are you really fighting about? Write about the fights you have had with your parents or friends and express your anger, hurt, and disappointment.

An Imagined Correspondence

Write your parents a letter in your less dominant hand. Begin with "Dear Mom" or "Dear Dad." You could tell them something that you are sad about and would like to have healed or you could express your gratitude to them.

Words of Praise

Imagine that you have received a letter from your parents telling you that they are proud of you for something you have accomplished. Allow them to express their love and pride in you in this imagined letter, that you receive with an open heart.

Acts of Love

What are the things that make you feel loved, cared about, or special? Keep an ongoing list of what makes you feel loved. Be sure to include the ways you nurture yourself. Who in your life gives you love?

A Kiss

Kisses are special and often memorable.
Write about your first kiss or a special kiss,
or write about your desire to kiss someone you
have yet to kiss.

Crushes

Write about your crushes. Is there anyone you can't stop thinking about? Are you able to talk to them or do you admire them from afar? What would you say to them if you could tell them what you felt.

Love Defined

Define true love. How do you know when you are in love? Describe your ideal relationship with a boyfriend or girlfriend. Write about how you would like to be treated and how you would treat them.

Love's Poetry

Express the love you feel for your family, friends, or someone special in a poem, letter, or card that you create and glue here.

Curiosity About My Sexuality

Write about your curiosity about or experience with sex and sexuality. Who or what has influenced your attitudes or curiosity about sex? Think about how you can be true to yourself without being pressured into doing something you're not comfortable with or ready to do.

Heartbreak

Write about a time when someone broke your heart. Allow yourself to feel all of your hurt, pain, and sadness. If you have any unfinished business with this person, allow yourself to express it now.

For Excellence

Give yourself an award that you truly deserve for an obstacle you have overcome, a habit you've broken, an area of growth, or an accomplishment.

In honor and recognition of your accomplishment, we hereby present

_____

(your name)

_____

with this award for

_____

For Excellence

In honor and recognition
of your accomplishment,
we hereby present

_____
(your name)

_____
with this award for

_____

Making Fun

Write about a time that someone made fun of you, ridiculed you, or belittled you. Describe how it affected you then and how it affects you now. Then write about a time you made fun of or belittled someone, consciously or unconsciously. Express your sadness, regret, or other feelings now.

Walking on the Wild Side

How has behavior ranging from swearing to drinking or using drugs affected you, your family, or your friends? Describe your own destructive behavior or that of those you know. How have these habits affected you and your relationships? What has happened as a result?

119

Popularity

Sometimes you have to look, act, or dress a certain way if you want to be popular. People can be cruel to those who don't fit in with their circle. How important is being popular to you? Can you be popular and be true to yourself? Do you feel accepted for who you are? Write about what fitting in means to you.

Hearts
with Hands

Sometimes people have difficulty asking for help. Identify the areas in your life where you could use help. Who could help you? How could you help yourself? Write a letter from your heart, asking for help.

Mistakes
I've Made
and Lessons
I've Learned

In life mistakes are inevitable. Make a list of mistakes you've made and the lessons you've learned. Keep an ongoing list of mistakes and lessons.

What Makes Your Heart Sing?

There are so many ways to have fun. What are the things that bring you joy, lift your spirit, and make you happy?

100 Dreams and Desires

List 100 dreams and desires you have. Write about what you yearn for. Name your heart's desires, and include specific items: family and home, school, work, personal and spiritual goals, dreams you have for those you love and for the world. To get what you want in life, you must first know what it is you desire. As your dreams come to pass, remember to check them off here. It is empowering to know you can create what you yearn for.

1. _____ ☐
2. _____ ☐
3. _____ ☐
4. _____ ☐
5. _____ ☐
6. _____ ☐
7. _____ ☐
8. _____ ☐
9. _____ ☐
10. _____ ☐
11. _____ ☐
12. _____ ☐
13. _____ ☐
14. _____ ☐
15. _____ ☐
16. _____ ☐
17. _____ ☐
18. _____ ☐

19. _____ ☐
20. _____ ☐
21. _____ ☐
22. _____ ☐
23. _____ ☐
24. _____ ☐
25. _____ ☐
26. _____ ☐
27. _____ ☐
28. _____ ☐
29. _____ ☐
30. _____ ☐
31. _____ ☐
32. _____ ☐
33. _____ ☐
34. _____ ☐
35. _____ ☐
36. _____ ☐
37. _____ ☐
38. _____ ☐
39. _____ ☐
40. _____ ☐
41. _____ ☐
42. _____ ☐
43. _____ ☐
44. _____ ☐
45. _____ ☐

46. _____ ☐
47. _____ ☐
48. _____ ☐
49. _____ ☐
50. _____ ☐
51. _____ ☐
52. _____ ☐
53. _____ ☐
54. _____ ☐
55. _____ ☐
56. _____ ☐
57. _____ ☐
58. _____ ☐
59. _____ ☐
60. _____ ☐
61. _____ ☐
62. _____ ☐
63. _____ ☐
64. _____ ☐
65. _____ ☐
66. _____ ☐
67. _____ ☐
68. _____ ☐
69. _____ ☐
70. _____ ☐
71. _____ ☐
72. _____ ☐

73. _____ ☐
74. _____ ☐
75. _____ ☐
76. _____ ☐
77. _____ ☐
78. _____ ☐
79. _____ ☐
80. _____ ☐
81. _____ ☐
82. _____ ☐
83. _____ ☐
84. _____ ☐
85. _____ ☐
86. _____ ☐
87. _____ ☐
88. _____ ☐
89. _____ ☐
90. _____ ☐
91. _____ ☐
92. _____ ☐
93. _____ ☐
94. _____ ☐
95. _____ ☐
96. _____ ☐
97. _____ ☐
98. _____ ☐
99. _____ ☐
100. _____ ☐

Money Matters

We all have a relationship with money. How are you similar to or different from your parents in the way you handle your money? Do you have difficulties or are you successful in your relationship with money? Write about the ways you either spend, save, or plan for your future. How could you make improvements?

Keeping
My Word

Learning to keep agreements is a first step towards a successful life. Do you keep your agreements with your parents and friends? Write about how you feel when others don't keep their promises to you.

Good Fortunes

In life we can often create our own good fortune. Glue an envelope on this page and save your good fortunes from fortune cookies. Write your own fortunes on slips of paper and glue or tuck them here.

137

Dreaming the Dream

Dreams can come true. The first step is in the imagining. Einstein said, "Imagination is more important than knowledge." Write about a dream, something you would love to do, be, or have if anything were possible. Describe your vision for your future.

For Your Continued Journey:
A Gift of More Exercises

E very day we have choices. Every day we continue to change and grow. Here are more exercises to help you to find yourself, be true to yourself, and create your dreams and heart's desires.

I Believe

Write a poem or a letter about your beliefs. Begin with "I believe."

Loving Myself

Write about how you could love yourself more.

Being Self-Conscious

Everyone is self–conscious about something. Describe what embarrasses you or causes you to feel self–conscious.

Time

Write about how you are currently spending your time. What do you do for fun? Is there anything you wish you had more time for?

My Feelings

Write of your most frequently felt feelings. Remember, we are the ones who choose. Write about what you would like to be feeling and what you are willing to do to create those feelings.

Respect

Who do you feel respects you as a person, and how do they show you respect? Describe the ways you experience respect or show disrespect in your life.

To Wait or Not to Wait

Describe how your own or someone else's sexual experiences or pregnancy have influenced you and your decision to have sex or wait.

Gossip

Many people have had devastating experiences with gossip. Sometimes rumors can hurt a reputation or damage a friendship. Write about how you deal with gossip. Do you participate or do you take a stand against it?

School

Write about your life at school.

Drama

Write about the drama you are creating in your life and how it keeps you from finding and being true to yourself.

Your Seeking Heart

Describe the state of your seeking heart. Often as we grow, we become kinder, more patient, and expand in our capacity to love. Make a list of the questions you've had or the answers you've found. Write a prayer, poem, or paragraph about your journey.

The Rules

Rules often keep us safe. What are the rules in your life? Do you follow the rules or do you tend to break them? Make a list of rules for yourself that would assist you in being your best.

Talking on the Phone

We maintain our connections with our friends by talking on the phone. Describe your experiences and frustrations with the telephone.

Dark Night of the Soul

A dark night of the soul is when life is difficult and we temporarily lose faith. Write about a time when you experienced a dark night of the soul. Express your pain, depression, or sadness. How did you get through it? What lessons have you learned?

Memories

Our hearts have their own memories. Our memories and our experiences make us who we are. What are some of your childhood memories? Describe everything that you can recall—the colors, sights, sounds, and emotions.

My Faith

When life challenges us and gives us more than we think we can bear, it is easy to lose faith. Make a list of all the things you have faith in. Sometimes recalling the things we trust or believe in with an absolute certainty gives us confidence in life.

Forgiving Myself

We are often our own harshest critics. Write a letter of forgiveness about something for which you have yet to forgive yourself.

Suicide

Have you or anyone you know ever thought about suicide? What prompted this thought? How did you overcome it or ask for help?

Vacations

Write about a memorable vacation that you've taken or a special vacation that you'd like to take.

Life's Frustrations

Express the frustrations you feel in your life. Describe the ways you currently handle frustration at home, school, and work. Unfortunately some people take their frustrations out on others. What do you do when you are frustrated?

Smoking

Write about your experience or a friend's experience with cigarettes and smoking. Have you or anyone you know experienced an addiction to smoking?

Driving

Write about your driving experiences as a passenger and/or a driver. Do you feel confident or scared on the road? Are you a reckless or a safe driver? Are you comfortable driving with your friends?

The Blame Game

Often it is easier to blame others than to take responsibility. Who are you blaming for your life's circumstances?

Green with Envy

Who or what makes you envious? Is anyone envious of you?

Your Parents' History

History can often repeat itself. Write about your parents' history. Describe how it has affected you, your values, choices, and the way you live your life.

Divorce

Write about how divorce has affected your life or the life of someone you know. Is there anything positive that has come out of this experience? Write about your true feelings.

Unique and Different Friends

Describe your unique and different friends. What have they brought to your life?

Safety

Many teenagers are experiencing violence in their lives and fearing for their safety. Describe your own experiences with violence, cruelty, or anything that has caused you to feel unsafe. Express what it will take for you to feel safe.

Trust

Whom can you trust? Whom do you trust? Create your own definition of trust and what makes a person trustworthy.

Tears

Tears are as important as laughter. What makes you sad? What tears haven't you cried yet. Write about the tears you are you holding back and why.

Windows to the Soul

What windows are opening or closing in your life? What are you passing through, going towards, or moving away from?

If I Knew I Could

If you knew you could, what would you do?

Feel free to use this page for gluing on
a pocket or envelope.

For information regarding Rose Offner's
books, tapes, lectures, workshops,
and consulting arrangements,
contact:

FROM THE INSIDE OUT
P.O. Box 2801
Castro Valley, CA 94546–0801
(510) 538–5074
Roseoffner@aol.com

Other Books by Rose Offner:
Journal to the Soul
Letters from the Soul
Journal to Intimacy

Please write to me with your stories,
experiences, and journal entries you're willing
to share.

Thank you,
Rose